My Pet Rabbit

My Pet Rabbit

by **Kristine I. Spangard**
photographs by **Andy King**

All About Pets

Lerner Publications Company • Minneapolis

To Katrina and Nicholas (and of course Brownie)—K.S.

Acknowledgments

The publisher would like to thank Dr. Curtis McDougall, Katrina Schubert, Nicholas Schubert, Sheri Sommers, and Kristine Spangard, who were photographed for this book. Thanks also to the East Lake Animal Clinic and Pet Central Station, Minneapolis, Minnesota, and to Dr. Barb Leppke.

Photos on p. 9 (top) & 51 reproduced by permission of the American Rabbit Breeders Association; p. 9 (center) American Harlequin Rabbit Club; p. 9 (bottom) Lop Rabbit Club; p. 10 (left) Norvia Behling. Photos on pp. 32, 47, & 57 by Jim Simondet/Independent Picture Service. Artwork on p. 24 by Laura Westlund.

Library of Congress Cataloging-in-Publication Data

Spangard, Kristine I.
  My pet rabbit / by Kristine I. Spangard ; photographs by Andy King.
    p.   cm. — (All about pets)
  Includes bibliographical references and index.
  Summary: Text and photographs follow a twelve-year-old girl as she learns about rabbits and how to care for one as a pet.
    ISBN 0–8225–2257–8 (hardcover—alk. paper)
    ISBN 0–8225–9795–0 (paperback—alk. paper)
    1. Rabbits—Juvenile literature. [1. Rabbits as pets. 2. Pets.]
  I. King, Andy, ill. II. Title. III. Series.
  SF453.2.S75   1997
  636.9'322—dc21   96–40245

Manufactured in the United States of America
1 2 3 4 5 6 — JR — 02 01 00 99 98 97

Contents

Rabbits don't make me sneeze...

My cello teacher has cats, so I know I'm allergic to them.

My name is Katrina, and I'm 12. I'd always wanted a pet. I thought it would be cool to have an animal as a friend. I could watch it grow up and get to know its personality. But with my allergies, I thought I wouldn't be able to have one. Furry animals, like dogs and cats and hamsters, make me sneeze. And I just can't get into fish or lizards. I wanted a soft, cuddly animal for a pet.

Then I went to my friend Beth's house for the first time. Beth has a bunny named Fuzzy. We played with Fuzzy for hours and my nose didn't even itch! As soon as I got home, I asked Mom if we could get a rabbit. They're soft and cute—quiet, too. Mom thinks that's important.

My little brother, Nicholas, has stuffed animals. We've never had a real animal for a pet, though.

When we went to the library that night, I looked up rabbits. I found so much information! I found out that rabbits live for 6 to 10 years. So if I got a baby rabbit this year, it would probably live until I was in college. That's a long time! I also learned that there are a lot of different kinds, or breeds, of rabbits. They come in too many colors to describe them all.

The smaller breeds are the most "hyper" or nervous. Even though some people choose small rabbits because they seem to be a better size for kids, they may be harder to handle. Medium breeds are usually calmer and friendlier. Large breeds also tend to be calm and friendly, but they need a lot more space than the smaller types. That ruled out a large rabbit for us.

The Right Rabbit for You

Here are some general characteristics of a few of the most popular breeds of pet rabbits.

Small breeds: *Under 5 pounds*

Netherland dwarf	Various colors, short ears
Polish	Under 3 pounds, tiny ears and big eyes, white, chocolate, or black
Holland lop	Various colors, lopping (drooping) ears

Medium breeds: *Approximately 4½ to 10 pounds*

Mini lop	Solid or broken colors, lopping ears
Dutch	Two-toned with white around shoulders and down middle of face
New Zealand white	White rabbit with pink ears and pink eyes
Harlequin	"Calico cat" of rabbits: one side of the face is dark with a light ear, the other side light with a dark ear; the rest of the body is usually striped

Large breeds: *Over 10 pounds*

French lop	About 12 pounds, lopping ears
English lop	Very long lopping ears (they drag on the ground), which can cause ear problems
Flemish giant	Some males are as large as 22 pounds!

Prices for rabbits can range from just a few dollars to over a hundred, depending on the type of rabbit. If you want to take your rabbit to shows or use them in 4-H projects, you should probably get a purebred rabbit.

The next day Mom came home from work with some good news. She told her friend at work that I wanted to get a rabbit. He has a pet rabbit in his apartment. He said he keeps the rabbit in a cage when he's not at home, so she doesn't get into mischief or get hurt. But he lets her out a lot, and she isn't messy. His rabbit even uses a litter box, like a cat!

Mom asked him if the rabbit was expensive. He said she cost about $10, and it didn't cost a lot to feed her. He got his rabbit from a breeder. He gave Mom the breeder's phone number.

Rabbits can live in people's houses pretty comfortably. Nicholas and I read about housetraining rabbits.

That night Mom called the breeder, whose name is Sheri. Sheri raises a kind of rabbit called a mini lop. *Lopping* means "drooping." The mini lop is a rabbit with cute, droopy ears. It's a mid-size breed.

Sheri told Mom we could come out to her place on Saturday. Two of her female rabbits had just had babies, so there were some little ones to see. They weren't ready to leave their mothers yet. But it was okay for us to look at them. Mom set up a time to go to Sheri's on Saturday, after my cello lesson. Then she handed the phone to me. "Why don't you talk to Sheri?" she said.

Nicholas wanted a pet as much as I did. He was excited that we might get a rabbit.

Housetraining a Rabbit

If you decide to have a "house rabbit," you may want to housetrain it. Start training when your rabbit is between 6 and 13 weeks old. You will need a cat litter box, litter, and a spray bottle filled with water or apple bitter water (available at drugstores). You will also need lots of patience.

When you first bring your rabbit home, place it in the cage you've prepared. Leave it alone, but watch to see where it urinates. Once a rabbit "scents" a spot, it will continue to use the same spot for the toilet.

Place the litter box over the spot your rabbit used for the toilet. The rabbit will then use the litter box as its bathroom! When you are sure the rabbit is using the litter box, you can start handling it and letting it out of the cage.

When your rabbit is outside the cage, watch it closely for any sign it has to use the litter box, such as lifting its tail. If your rabbit does go outside the litter box, spray it with the water bottle and return it to the cage. Clean the spot thoroughly so no trace of the scent will tempt the rabbit to use that spot again. Be patient and never hit or yell at your rabbit.

In about three weeks, you should be able to leave the door to the cage open whenever you are home with the rabbit. Be sure to return it to the cage whenever you will be out of the house, even for a minute. Loose rabbits can be destructive. They will often chew on electrical cords and furniture.

If you catch your rabbit using another spot in the house for a litter box, spray the spot with apple bitters. The rabbit should not return to that spot. Once in a while, rabbits leave small droppings on the floor. Be sure to clean them up immediately, or the rabbit may begin to use that spot for a litter box.

I wrote my questions for the breeder on our computer. There was so much I didn't know about rabbits yet.

I could tell Sheri really liked her rabbits and knew a lot about them. She said I should make a list of questions to ask her on Saturday. So after I said good-bye, I got busy. By Friday night, my list looked like this:

How do I hold a rabbit?

What is the best place to keep a rabbit?

What does a rabbit eat?

Does a rabbit need exercise?

Do rabbits need any special equipment?

Why don't rabbits make me sneeze?

I got pretty good at holding them...

Sheri was waiting for us and ready to show us her rabbits.

On Saturday my mom, my brother, Nicholas, and I went to Sheri's place. When we got there, I was surprised by how it looked. I guess I thought that Sheri would live on a farm. But she lived in a normal house in the suburbs. The rabbit shed was in her backyard, next to the garage. It was a hot day, and fans were going full-blast inside the rabbit shed.

Inside the shed, three rows of rabbit cages were stacked on top of each other. I had never seen so many rabbits all at once! They all had droopy lop ears. But they were a bunch of different colors.

The mother rabbits, called does, shared their cages with their babies, called kittens. Each adult rabbit had its own cage.

The rabbits looked sleepy, but they came to the front of their cages. I guess they had to check us out, too.

Sheri told us that rabbits need their own space to feel safe. Also, the males—called bucks—will push, scratch, or bite the does. Sheri only puts them together when she wants them to breed.

We learned that rabbits have babies almost year-round. Each litter can have as many as 10 kittens. So if you have two or more rabbits of different sexes, you should keep them apart or have them sterilized ("fixed" so they don't have babies). Otherwise you'll have a very large rabbit family, very quickly!

Sheri took out a few rabbits, one at a time. She said rabbits become friendlier the more you hold them.

I just wanted one rabbit anyway. I was glad to hear that rabbits can be happy living alone. They like company, Sheri said, but human company suits them fine.

Sheri opened the cages with the baby bunnies in them. All the babies were so cute! At first we just looked and petted them a little. Then Sheri asked if we wanted to hold one. That was my first question—"How do I hold a rabbit?"

We petted the rabbits while Sheri held them.

Nicholas had a little trouble holding this rabbit. Nicholas's hands aren't very big yet.

The babies were just three weeks old. They were about as big as my hand. They were easy to hold, just like a little earmuff. The bigger ones looked like a handful—an armful even! Sheri told us two *S* words—*startle* and *security*—that would help us remember how to pick up a rabbit. *Startle* reminds you not to startle the rabbit. A startled rabbit will run. Or, if it's cornered, it may bite or scratch you. You should reach for it from the front or side, down on its level where it can see you.

The second *S* word, *security*, means you should hold a rabbit so it feels safe and secure. If a rabbit doesn't feel secure, it will struggle and kick its legs. The best way to make a rabbit feel secure when you pick it up is to support its rear end.

Sheri showed us a few different holds. My favorite one you do with the rabbit facing you. You put one hand under the rabbit's rib cage. Your other hand goes under the rabbit's rear end. Another way to lift a rabbit is by the nape of its neck. You have to be careful! With one hand, hold the loose skin at the back of its neck. Keep your other hand under the rabbit's rear. Lift the rabbit back, with its feet in front of its face.

This rabbit seemed a little scared. But I held it close, and it didn't kick.

Sheri told us to never, ever lift a rabbit by its ears. You could hurt the rabbit that way. She also taught us an easy way to stop a rabbit from squirming. All you do is cover its eyes with your hand. The rabbit should calm down. To put a rabbit down, lower its bottom first. If you lower it head first, it will probably jump out of your arms. Then the rabbit might get hurt or run away.

Handling the rabbits made me wonder again why I don't seem to be allergic to them. I asked Sheri if she knew the reason. She wasn't really sure. She said allergies to furry animals are usually caused by their dander—dry flakes of skin in the fur. Rabbits also have dander, just like other furry animals. She tells people to keep their rabbits clean and groomed, just to be safe.

Sheri showed us a trick for handling a rabbit. Cover its eyes, and it will calm down.

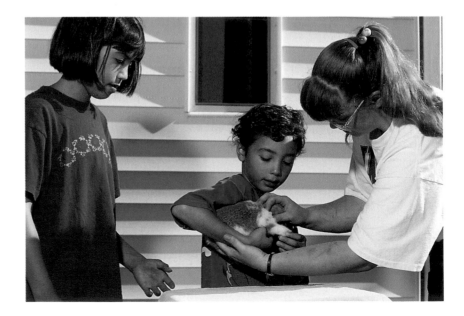

A rabbit uses its teeth and tongue to comb gunk out of its fur. Sheri said this can make a rabbit sick—hair balls form in its stomach. The rabbit won't throw up hair balls like a cat would, but a rabbit with hair balls will stop eating and drinking. If you think your rabbit has hair balls, take it to a veterinarian. To keep your rabbit from getting hair balls in the first place, groom it every day.

Sheri showed us an easy way to groom rabbits. First she sprayed our hands with water. Then we petted the rabbits. The loose hair came off and stuck to our hands.

Grooming the rabbits was as easy as petting them. If you groom a rabbit regularly, it won't get hair balls.

We took the rabbits outside to groom them. I think they liked being out of their cages.

I asked Sheri the next question on my list: "What is the best place to keep a rabbit?" Sheri said she liked raised wire cages best. When a rabbit goes to the bathroom, its droppings fall through the wire bottom. They are caught in the tray underneath. You can bag the droppings and throw them away with the rest of your garbage. Or the waste pellets can be used for fertilizer on the garden or lawn. The tray should be emptied two or more times a week. You should scrub the tray with soap and water before you put it back.

I saw an empty rabbit hutch in Sheri's neighbor's yard. When I asked Sheri about it, she said her neighbor used to raise rabbits, too. He was looking for someone to buy the hutch. I could just picture it in our backyard.

Since we live in Minnesota, where the winters are really cold, I wondered if rabbits could live outside all year. Sheri said it wasn't a problem. In winter, rabbits grow thick, warm winter coats to protect them from the cold. But you need to *be sure* to provide a safe place for an outdoor rabbit. The cage or hutch must be off the ground, out of the reach of dogs and cats. A shady spot is the best, because rabbits don't like bright sun.

Wire cages don't look comfortable, but they're healthy for rabbits. The rabbits get fresh air, and their cages stay pretty clean.

Outdoor Rabbits

If you keep your rabbit outside, you must be sure it stays dry. When a rabbit gets wet, the fur can no longer trap heat next to the rabbit's body. The rabbit may freeze if temperatures are very cold. To protect your rabbit from rain and snow, give it a sturdy, waterproof shelter. This shelter can be inside the cage, or built onto one end. Just be sure to check the shelter daily for ice. Rabbits will sometimes urinate inside their boxes, and the urine may freeze inside.

If you bring an outside rabbit inside during the winter, it will lose its heavy, protective winter coat. Then the rabbit must stay inside until temperatures are constantly in the 50s again. Otherwise, it will not survive.

Give your rabbit warm water to drink when it's cold outside. Not only does warm water help rabbits stay a bit warmer, but it takes longer to freeze into ice. It will freeze, though, so replace the water bottle often.

Normally, rabbits have a harder time living with heat than cold. They do not perspire like people do. Rabbits get rid of extra body heat through their ears, and by panting. To make your rabbit comfortable in hot weather, you can make it a mini-refrigerator. Freeze water in an old plastic gallon container. When temperatures rise above 80 degrees, put the container in the rabbit's cage. The rabbit will curl up around it and press its ears close to cool off.

Rabbits need extra salt in hot weather. You can buy spools of salt at a pet store.

I asked the next two questions on my list together. "Does a rabbit need any special exercise or any special equipment?" I was thinking of my friend who has a gerbil. There's an exercise wheel inside its cage.

Sheri said that a rabbit mainly needs to be active inside its cage. Sometimes she takes her rabbits outside on a leash. They like to sniff and explore the yard. They also like to eat fresh leaves and green grass. Sheri tries to keep them from nibbling too much. A little of that stuff won't hurt them. But if they eat a lot, they will get sick. Also, many common plants are poisonous to rabbits.

Sheri showed us how to put a harness on a rabbit. Then she hooked a leash to the harness and let the rabbit hop on the grass.

Rabbits can eat from dishes, like dogs and cats do. You can buy food for rabbits at a pet store.

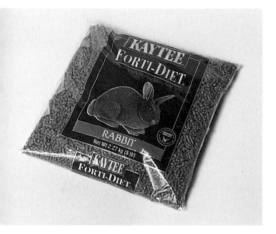

Rabbits are nibblers by nature, Sheri said. One special thing a rabbit needs is something hard to chew on. Rabbits' front teeth never stop growing. If they get too long, the rabbit can't chew food or close its mouth any more. Chewing wood keeps their front teeth worn down. You can use chunks of unpainted, untreated wood (the kind that isn't soaked in any preservative). Or you can give your rabbit twigs and sticks from your yard.

I asked Sheri what rabbits eat. She said rabbits don't eat meat, but they eat vegetables just like people do. She also feeds her rabbits hay and a special rabbit food that contains fiber and nutrients, like vitamins. Sheri feeds her rabbits twice a day—once in the morning and once in the evening.

All of a sudden, we heard banging noises coming from inside the shed. We went in to see what it was. "Look," Nicholas said. "One of the rabbits is playing with a can!"

"That's Beatrice," Sheri said. Sheri told us that her rabbits like to play with toys sometimes. But soft toys don't work—rabbits chew them to shreds. Beatrice's favorite toy is a tuna can with its ends cut out, with no sharp edges. Some rabbits like a tennis ball or just a wood chunk to push around their cages. Sam, another one of Sheri's rabbits, even plays catch with her. He stops the tennis ball and rolls it back.

All the rabbits were awake now. Some were playing with toys inside their cages.

We had fun outside with the rabbits. I think Mom was starting to like rabbits, too.

We took Sam outside to play catch in the yard. After a minute, a truck roared by. Sam took off toward the shed. Luckily he was on a leash and didn't run very fast. Sheri said her rabbits usually come back to her when they are out exploring. But they might run in any direction if they are startled.

I'd asked all the questions on my list. It was getting late, too. We thanked Sheri for showing us the rabbits, and we headed home.

In the car, Mom asked, "Well, how did you like the rabbits?"

"I really liked them! And I learned a lot!" I knew I could take care of a rabbit. I just didn't know if I really wasn't allergic to them. Mom thought I should find out before we got our pet.

The bunnies had to stay with their mother...

The next morning we looked up the animal science department at the university. We found the name of a professor in the telephone book. "Okay," Mom said. "I'll give her a call to get you started. Then you take over."

I asked the professor why I don't seem to be allergic to rabbits. She told me there could be a couple of reasons. One, I'm simply not allergic to rabbits! Two, I haven't been around rabbits much in my life, and my allergy hasn't developed. I could become allergic in a few years, when I've been around rabbits more often.

If you're allergic to your rabbit, you can try giving it a bath with special soap. Rabbits don't need baths, though. They keep themselves clean.

An outdoor hutch would
be best for my allergies.
Mom said we could get
the one we'd seen.

I hung up the phone and told Mom what the professor said. Mom could tell I was disappointed. She mentioned the hutch we saw at Sheri's house. We could keep a rabbit outside, she said. That way the rabbit's hair and dander wouldn't be in the house. It would probably take a lot longer for me to develop an allergy. Or it might not happen at all.

"But you would have to go outside to take care of it," Mom said. "Rain or shine, hot or cold."

"It would be worth it," I said.

"Well, you've really done your homework on rabbits," she said. "Okay. We can get a bunny."

We called Sheri and told her the good news. She reminded us that the bunnies needed to be with their mother for another week. I asked her about the hutch. She said her neighbor still wanted to sell it, so I told her we would buy it.

Before we got our rabbit, Mom picked up the hutch. We put it in the backyard right next to the house. The spot was mostly sheltered from wind, rain, and direct sunlight. We scrubbed the whole hutch with water and a little bit of bleach, then rinsed it with the hose. We also cleaned the food holder and water bottle that came with the hutch.

Some food and water holders have wire hooks on the back. They hook to the mesh of a cage.

Cagey Rabbits

When deciding on the size of your cage, allow ¾ square foot (81 square inches) of floor space for every pound your rabbit will weigh as an adult. For example, a mid-size rabbit will weigh approximately six pounds when fully grown: 6 pounds × ¾ square feet = 4½ square feet of floor space

This translates into a standard cage size of 24 inches by 30 inches by 18 inches high. Bigger rabbits require more space. (Fifteen-pound rabbits need more than twice as much space!) And, of course, smaller ones need less. Prices can range from $5 for a small used cage all the way up to $90 for a deluxe model. The average price is around $30-$50.

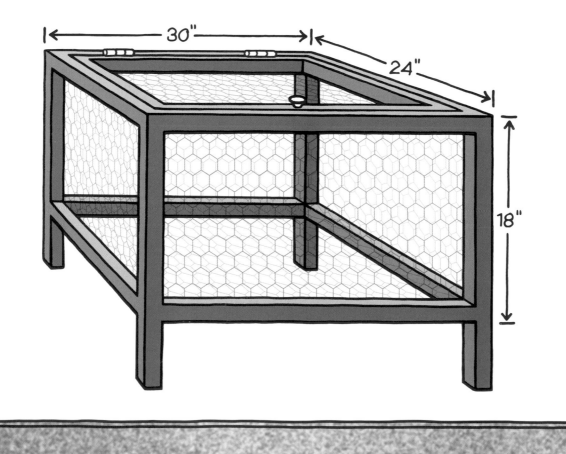

After that we went to the pet store. We bought some rabbit food that was the same brand Sheri feeds her rabbits. She had told us that any change to a new brand should be done gradually. The food cost about $12. It was a big bag that we figured would last four to six months. We also bought a bag of hay, a harness, a leash, and some claw trimmers for cutting the rabbit's nails.

At home, I checked the tools in the garage. I made sure we had a small shovel to scoop up the rabbit's droppings. Mom cleared some space under our kitchen sink to keep the food.

We hooked up the water bottle to the door of the hutch. We also put some wood chunks and a bright green tennis ball in the hutch. It looked homey and comfortable for a rabbit. The hard part was next— waiting for the day we could finally get our rabbit.

Mom was happy that the supplies didn't cost a lot. I was hoping we could buy a leash and harness, and we did.

34

He needed time to get used to us...

Nicholas and I could
hardly wait to go back
to Sheri's.

On Saturday morning I jumped out of bed. This
was bunny day! Since it was only 6:30, I tried to be
quiet. But I must have made too much noise,
because Nicholas came to my room a few seconds
later. He was also too excited to sleep, so we
played card games until breakfast time. Before we
left, we filled our bunny's bowl with food. We also
filled his bottle with water.

At Sheri's, we were surprised to see how much the babies had grown in just two weeks. They had been about five inches long when we first saw them. Now they were about eight inches long. Their coats were still shiny and beautiful. Their eyes looked bright. They were all so cute and cuddly! I wasn't sure I could pick just one.

I held most of the bunnies, one at a time. Finally I picked a dark brownish black one with gray feet and tummy. He looked clean and healthy. He wasn't sneezing or scratching. His fur was fluffy and smooth. He seemed the calmest and most beautiful to us.

It was hard to pick a favorite, but I liked this rabbit best.

My rabbit looked a little worried. I told him I was taking him to a nice, new home.

While Mom paid Sheri, I held my bunny in my lap. Sheri had put a harness on him, just in case. But I didn't have any trouble holding him. I remembered the lesson we had in holding rabbits.

I petted him gently on top of his head, between his eyes, and behind his ears. I talked to him quietly so he would get used to my voice. I also called him by his name—I had already decided to name him Brownie.

Sheri gave us a cardboard box for Brownie to sit in on the way home. She explained that the box would make Brownie feel safe. The box had a lid, and it was small and dark, like a rabbit house. If he couldn't see out, he wouldn't try to run away.

We promised Sheri we would call and let her know how Brownie was doing. She also said we should call if we had any questions or problems.

We lowered him into the box, bottom first, and closed the lid. We put the box on the backseat of the car. I sat on one side, and Nicholas was on the other. Mom drove slowly so Brownie wouldn't get thrown around inside the box.

Brownie didn't mind the box, but the car scared him. I petted him to keep him calm.

Brownie wasn't jumping out of the box, so we let him sit and look around.

Home at last! First we set the closed box on the grass next to the hutch. We opened the box's lid, but Brownie didn't move—he seemed scared. So we let him stay in the box for a while, while we watched him.

Nicholas watched Brownie while I opened the hutch.

Sheri had told us we should leave Brownie alone for a couple of days. He would need some time to adjust to his new home. Then he would be curious and would want to check us out. After this, we could start to play with him.

Until then, we just needed to give him food and water twice a day. We also needed to be around so he would see us and get used to us. I had read in the rabbit-care books that he would need time to get used to the way we smell, too.

I don't think Brownie wanted to be held just then. He seemed so scared!

I lifted Brownie out of his box, and he started kicking a little. I was worried that if he kicked too hard I'd drop him. So I petted Brownie's head and covered his eyes with my hand. He stopped kicking and I held him until he seemed calmer. Nicholas wanted to hold him. I let him for a minute, then I put Brownie inside his cage. As soon as I set him down, Brownie hopped to a back corner.

We knew rabbits are startled by loud sounds, but we thought Brownie might like some quiet music. I played a few tapes of classical music out the window so Brownie could hear them.

When we took Brownie out for the first time, it was just for half an hour. Nicholas and I sat on the ground with Brownie. First he sat in my lap, then in Nicholas's. We thought he needed some grooming. We sprayed our hands with water. Then we rubbed his fur until all the loose hairs came off.

Brownie stayed in one corner a long time. I knew it would be a while before he got used to us.

When I fed Brownie that evening, he seemed to want attention again. I petted and played with him for a longer time. The next day I took him out into the yard on a harness for some fun and exploring. It was a good thing I had the harness—some birds suddenly flew by, and Brownie almost took off!

Brownie seemed to love being outdoors. A couple times he tried to eat some green grass. I caught him and gave him some twigs and dry leaves instead. He didn't seem to mind. I could tell we were becoming good friends.

The next day, Brownie came to the front of the cage on his own.

It was time for a checkup...

I knew that to keep Brownie healthy, I had to clean his cage, keep him dry, and keep him out of drafts and very hot weather. He also needed a healthy diet. But Sheri said we should take Brownie to a veterinarian for a checkup as soon as he had gotten used to us. So about two weeks after we brought him home, we took him to see Dr. McDougall, a vet in our neighborhood.

When we took Brownie to his checkup, he was about two months old.

Dr. McDougall explained how he would examine Brownie. He said he would start by checking Brownie's coat, eyes, ears, nose, and teeth. We told Dr. McDougall that we'd checked these things when we chose Brownie. "Hey, that's great," he said. "Then you probably know what to watch for so that he doesn't get sick." Anything different or unusual can be a sign of disease.

Brownie looked nervous. I was a little nervous, too. Going to the vet was new for both of us.

Dr. McDougall asked us about Brownie's cage. He also wanted to know what kind of food Brownie eats.

We told the doctor that Brownie was a friendly, calm bunny. He ate the amount of food we gave him (about a quarter cup of pellets twice a day, plus lots of greens—like lettuce, fresh spinach, parsley, and carrot tops). He also drank lots of water, especially when it was hot outside.

We buy timothy hay at the pet store and feed it to Brownie every day.

We told Dr. McDougall that we give Brownie a special treat every day. We discovered that he really likes pears. We often gave Brownie a slice of pear with his other food.

He said that sounded fine, as long as we didn't give Brownie the pear seeds. (Pear seeds are poisonous to rabbits.) It's good to give your rabbit fresh food every day. Greens are the best. An average-size rabbit should have a heaping cup of greens at every meal. Rabbits also like thick slices of carrots and parsnips, or fruit—like apple slices, grapes, and strawberries.

"Don't give your rabbit sweets or junk food, though," Dr. McDougall said. "Too much of that is really dangerous for rabbits." He also said we should give him lots of timothy hay every day—as much as he wanted.

The vet said Brownie's teeth looked great!

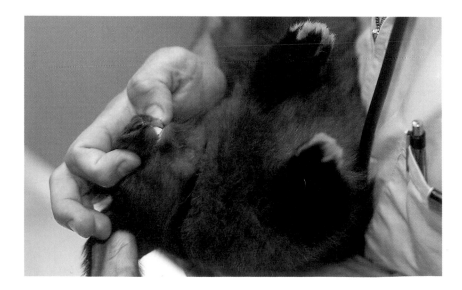

Rabbit Food

Rabbit pellets sold in pet stores contain some fiber and nutrients. You can feed your rabbit ¼ cup of pellets each day, per 5 pounds of body weight. (An average-size, 10-pound rabbit would eat ½ cup of pellets a day.) You should also give your rabbit as much hay as it will eat. But to be healthy, rabbits need fresh food. A varied diet is best.

Add new foods to a rabbit's diet gradually. Try feeding your rabbit one new food from this list every 3 to 5 days. If any new food makes your rabbit sick with diarrhea, stop giving the rabbit that particular food.

Greens & Vegetables:

Feed at least 1 heaping cup of greens and vegetables each day, per 5 pounds of body weight.

Spinach	Mustard greens	Carrot tops
Celery	Dandelion greens	Beet roots
Peas	and flowers	Sugar beets
Beans	(*not* from a	Parsnips
Beet tops	lawn treated	Parsley
Kale	with chemical	Alfalfa (in small
Endive	fertilizer or	quantities, just
Carrots	pesticides)	as a snack)

Fruits:

Feed 1 tablespoon of fruit each day, per 5 pounds of body weight.

Apples	Cherries	Melons
Grapes	Raspberries	Mangoes
Pears	Blueberries	Peaches
Oranges	Papayas	Tomatoes
Strawberries	Pineapples	

The vet looked in Brownie's ears with a little light.

The doctor checked Brownie's weight and temperature, listened to his breathing and his heart, and felt his tummy and sides. He said he could feel that all the inside organs—like the stomach, liver, and kidneys—were the right size and shape for a rabbit. He can sometimes tell if a rabbit has a hair ball in his stomach by feeling his tummy. But he said Brownie's insides felt okay.

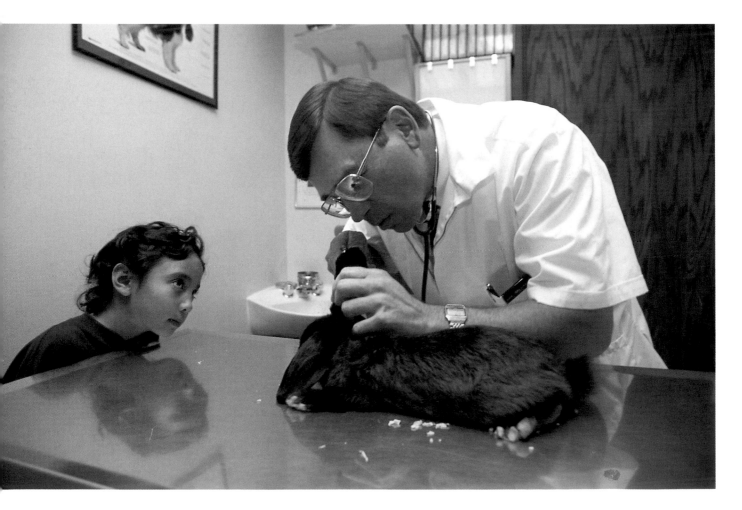

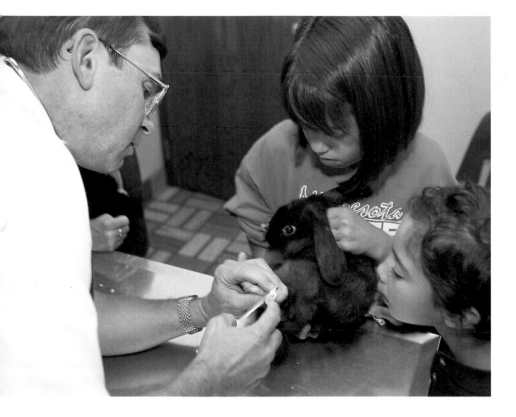

Brownie squirmed and kicked when we clipped his nails. But when we got him to stay still, it wasn't too hard.

Then Dr. McDougall showed us how to clip Brownie's toenails. Rabbits have a vein inside each nail, and it hurts them if you cut into it. You can hold the nail up to a light and see where the vein ends. Then cut off the nail about one-quarter inch longer than the vein. Dr. McDougall cut a few of Brownie's nails while I held him. I clipped the rest myself. The vet said I should clip Brownie's nails about once every other month.

Then Dr. McDougall told us about some illnesses rabbits can get. Sometimes rabbits get colds just like we do, and they sneeze and have runny noses.

Rabbits also can get ear mites—bugs that get into their ears. A rabbit with ear mites will scratch its ears a lot. Sometimes rabbits get a disease called conjunctivitis, and their eyes look itchy and red. If your rabbit shows any signs of a cold, ear mites, or conjunctivitis, you should take it to a vet.

Something else we need to watch for is sore feet. A rabbit's feet get sore from standing on a wire cage. A medicine call Preparation H can help. It's sold at drugstores. Just rub a little on the pads of your rabbit's feet.

A serious problem the vet warned us about was diarrhea. We already knew that rabbits can get diarrhea from a bad diet. It can also be caused by an infection, and a veterinarian needs to treat it.

The bottoms of a rabbit's feet don't have much fur for padding. We made sure Brownie's feet didn't look sore.

Spaying and Neutering

Spaying and neutering are operations in which an animal's sex organs are removed. The operation will make him or her unable to make babies. Single pet rabbits cannot produce unwanted baby bunnies. But there are still some good reasons to have your rabbit spayed or neutered.

Non-neutered adult bucks mark their territory by spraying urine. They may also be aggressive and fight for their territory. Neutered males are calmer.

Adult does that have not been spayed may have false pregnancies. This condition causes them to pull out lots of their belly and chest fur, to make a nest. Also, females that are not spayed have more health problems and diseases. And they can become aggressive and bite when they are not regularly bred.

The ideal time to have a rabbit neutered or spayed is between 4 and 6 months for smaller breeds to over 8 months for the larger ones. Be sure to talk to your vet to learn the best time to perform the operation for your rabbit. He or she can describe the operation to you, and discuss the risks, benefits, and costs.

When we got home, I gave Brownie a treat for being a good patient.

The last thing we discussed with Dr. McDougall was when to bring Brownie back to be neutered. We wanted him to have this operation so he wouldn't begin spraying urine to mark his territory around our house. And neutered rabbits are calmer and friendlier when they grow up. Brownie was only about two months old. We had to wait another four months, until he was full grown.

CHAPTER 6

He's a member of the family...

Routine is very important to a rabbit's health. Both Sheri and the vet said that change can cause a rabbit stress. So we try to do things with him at the same time every day.

First thing in the morning, I go outside to make sure Brownie is okay. I give him fresh food and a handful of timothy hay. I check the water bottle and refill it if the water is low. Then I pet Brownie and talk to him until it's time for my breakfast.

When I leave Brownie, I make sure his cage is closed and the combination lock locked. That way he won't get out and hurt himself, and no strangers can hurt him or take him.

Mom helped feed Brownie the first couple weeks. After that, I could do it myself.

I try to get Brownie to play every day, but some days he's not interested. Sometimes even rabbits need time to themselves.

When Nicholas and I come home from school, we like playing with Brownie. He is more active by this time of day. We can tell if he wants attention, because he will start jumping around. He comes to the front of the cage when he sees us. Sometimes we take him out. But if it's too hot or rainy, we leave him in his hutch and play games with him. Brownie's favorite games are tossing his tennis ball and chewing on his stick.

Once in a while, he's just not in the mood to play. He stays in the back of his cage when we come to check on him. As long as he is not sick or hurt, we just leave him alone.

Every evening after our supper, we give Brownie more food and water and a few last pats goodnight. Since rabbits are active at night, we have to take any noisy toys from his cage, like the tuna can. Otherwise, we can hear the noise through the window.

About once a week, I clean out all the droppings under the cage. I put them in the compost pile. Then I spread fresh cedar chips under Brownie's cage. I've heard you can use cat litter under your rabbit cage, too. Mom has had to remind me to do this cleanup a few times, because it's a job I don't like. But it's part of having a rabbit.

Cedar chips smell good. They also make the ground underneath the cage look neater.

We don't take Brownie out on the hottest days. He keeps cool inside his cage with a container of ice.

On nice days, we put on Brownie's harness and leash. Then we take him for a walk in the yard. Brownie usually finds something interesting, like a great chewing stick. He doesn't try to run away very much anymore. But we are still careful to watch him all the time. His leash gets tangled up sometimes. And I've caught him trying to chew through the leash.

Brownie usually tries to eat grass or plants in the yard. I have to stop him by keeping him moving, but I don't yell at him or hit him or yank him. I just spray him with a little water to let him know he did something he wasn't supposed to.

Poisonous Plants

Rabbits love to chew on plants. But pet rabbits do not know by instinct that many plants are poisonous. To be safe, don't feed your rabbit any plants you are unsure of. And keep your rabbit away from any houseplants or plants in your yard or garden. Below is a list of some of the plants and plant parts that are poisonous to rabbits.

Acorns	Eucalyptus	Oak
Almonds	Gladiola	Peach pits
Apple seeds	Hyacinth bulbs	Pear seeds
Apricot pits	Hydrangea	Peony
Asparagus fern	Iris	Philodendron
Azalea	Ivy	Plum pits
Bleeding heart	Jack-in-the-pulpit	Poinsettia
Carnations	Jonquil	Pothos
Cherry pits	Lily of the valley	Rhododendron
Clematis	Milkweed	Rhubarb leaves
Creeping Charlie	Mistletoe	Skunk cabbage
Daffodil bulbs	Mustards	Tomato leaves
Daisy	Nutmeg	Tulip bulbs

This is only a partial list. For a more complete list, contact a poison control center.

Once while Brownie was on the leash, Nicholas got the idea to let him play in the sandbox. It was sunny that day. Once Brownie was in the sand, he started burrowing down. He flattened his body on the sand, trying to make a little shelter from the heat. He ended up under the wooden seat at one corner of the box. Just his feet were sticking out.

Last winter was very long and cold. A few days, the temperature stayed below zero all day long. We put a box and some pieces of towels in Brownie's cage for extra warmth. We had to keep checking his water bottle, too. When the water froze, the ice split the bottle open. We had to buy two or three new bottles that winter. And we always kept an extra bottle on hand.

Brownie has really gotten used to us and become a good friend.

A rabbit is a good pet for my family and me.

We've had Brownie for over a year, and he's really become a member of the family. He's been a best buddy to Nicholas and me. He makes us feel loved when we're sad, just by being there. Touching his soft fur and seeing his cute face always make us feel better. And we are sharing the responsibility and fun of taking care of him. We like to do a great job, because Brownie is so wonderful to us. Like his name, he is a sweet chocolatey brown bunny!

Glossary

Allergies (*al*-er-jees): conditions in which a person becomes sick, gets a rash, sneezes, or has trouble breathing after coming in contact with something that is not harmful to most people

Diarrhea (dye-uh-*ree*-uh): a condition in which an animal has runny stools (poops). Diarrhea is a sign of an unhealthy diet or an illness.

Ear mites: tiny bugs that can live inside some animals' ears. Ear mites are arachnids (uh-*rak*-nids), related to spiders.

Hair balls: clumps of hair that form in the stomach of an animal that licks its fur

Housetrained: trained to live in a house. Rabbits that are housetrained use a litter box.

Instinct (*in*-stinkt): a way of feeling or acting that is natural to an animal, rather than learned

Purebred (*pyoor*-bred): having ancestors of the same breed

Territory (*ter*-uh-tor-ee): an area chosen by an animal as its own

Timothy hay: blades of a grass plant called timothy that have been mowed and dried for animals to eat

Resources

American Rabbit Breeders Association (ARBA)
Box 426
Bloomington, IL 61702
309-664-7500
e-mail: ARBAMAIL@aol.com
A nationwide organization of people who raise rabbits.

Delta Society
289 Perimeter Road East
Renton, WA 98055
(206) 226-7357
An international organization for studying human-
animal relationships. Will send a list of books on
animal topics.

Humane Society of the U.S.
2100 L Street NW
Washington, DC 20037
Free tips on caring for birds, dogs, cats, and small
mammals.

Tree House Animal Foundation
784-5488, Wed.-Sun.
(773) 784-5577, Hotline open 7 days a week.
Specializes in behavior questions. Caller pays long-
distance charges, but consultation is free.

For Further Reading

Barrie, Anmarie. *Rabbits For Those Who Care.* Neptune City, NJ: T.F.H. Publications, 1994.

Evans, Mark. *Rabbit.* (Eyewitness Handbooks.) New York: Dorling Kindersley, 1992.

Lee, Barbara. *Working with Animals.* Minneapolis: Lerner, 1996.

Oxford Scientific Films. *The Wild Rabbit.* New York: Putnam, 1980.

Savage, Stephen. *Rabbit.* New York: Thomson Learning, 1995.

Searle, Nancy. *Your Rabbit: A Kid's Guide to Raising and Showing.* Pownal, VT: Storey Communications, 1992.

Sproule, Anna. *Rabbits.* New York: Bookwright Press, 1988.

Staub, Frank. *America's Prairies.* Minneapolis: Carolrhoda, 1994.

Trost, Lucille Wood. *Biography of a Cottontail.* New York: Putnam, 1971.

Index

ABOUT THE AUTHOR

Kristine Spangard grew up in a small town in northern Illinois, where she loved to bike around town with her friends, dance, swim in the lake, and climb trees. Kristine still dances, climbs rock walls as well as trees, and swims in the lakes of Minneapolis with her two children. She holds an M.S. in Technical Communications, and she works for a high-tech laser company.

ABOUT THE PHOTOGRAPHER

Andy King is a native of Boulder, Colorado, and a graduate of Colorado State University. Andy has traveled around the world as a documentary and corporate photographer, and he has worked as a photographer at newspapers in Minnesota and Texas. He lives with his wife, Patricia, and their daughter in St. Paul, Minnesota, where he enjoys mountain biking and playing basketball.